# THE RAVEN

## BY EDGAR ALLEN POE

## ILLUSTRATED BY

## GUSTAVE DORÉ

COVER ILLUSTRATION BY  PANTELIS POLITAKOS

DESIGN, LAYOUT, AND IMAGE EDITING BY MOSES NYUIADZI

# THE RAVEN

Originally published in 1884 by Harper Brothers New York City

Re-published 2020 by SLG Publishing
www.slgpubs.com
isbn 978-1-59362-297-8
44 Race Street San Jose CA 95126
Cover © 2020 SLG Publishing

# FOREWORD

The Raven is maybe the one work by Edgar Allan Poe that best reflects his tortured and convoluted life. His alcoholism and depression are well-documented and his struggles in life were the fuel for his dark and horrific literature. One of the best-known poems in the English speaking world, The Raven was originally published in 1845, Poe being paid the princely sum of $9.00 for it to appear in The American Review. An immediate success The Raven would appear in several publications across the United States including the New York Tribune (February 4, 1845), Broadway Journal (vol. 1, February 8, 1845), Southern Literary Messenger (vol. 11, March 1845), Literary Emporium (vol. 2, December 1845), Saturday Courier, 16 (July 25, 1846), and the Richmond Examiner (September 25, 1849). It has also appeared in numerous anthologies, starting with Poets and Poetry of America edited by Rufus Wilmot Griswold in 1847.

Gustav Doré was a French illustrator, printmaker, and sculptor who worked primarily in engraving and woodcut illustration. Having previously illustrated works by such literary titans as Dante, Balzac, Milton, Coleridge, Tennyson, and Lord Byron, Doré created a series of stark, beautifully haunting steel-plate engravings for a special edition of The Raven. It became his final legacy — Doré died shortly after completing the illustrations, at the age of fifty-one, and this exquisite edition was posthumously published in 1884.

The book you are reading uses scans from one of the many versions of the original book but has been digitally enhanced to make for a darker, more contemporary look. Many of the original aspects of the woodcut illustration have been lost however we feel that our finished product retains the moody and dark imagery Doré was going for while eliminating many of the artifacts and imperfections that are commonly seen in reprints like these. The cover is an all-new painting based on the original cover and is a full-color illustration which again retains the mood and look of the classic Doré illustrations while giving it a more contemporary look that is well-suited for the modern printing process.

# OTHER CLASSICS FROM SLG PUBLISHING

**Grosses Betes & Petites Betes (Big Beasts and Little Beasts):
Big Beasts and Little Beasts by Andre Helle**
isbn - 978-159362-291-6 - $11.95


**The Nine Lives of a Cat by Charles Bennett**
isbn - 978-1-59362-274-9 - $4.99

**Death and Burial of Poor Cock Robin by H.L. STEPHENS**
isbn - 978-1-59362-275-6  $4.99

**Baby's Own Aesop by Illustrated by Walter Crane**
isbn - 978-1-59362-273-2  $9.95

# GUSTAVE DORÉ

**Paul Gustave Louis Christophe Doré** was a French artist, print-maker, illustrator, comics artist, caricaturist, and sculptor who worked primarily with wood-engraving. Born in Strasbourg in 1832, Doré was creating art by age 5, producing drawings that were mature beyond his years. Seven years later, he began carving in stone.

At the age of 15, Doré began his career working as a caricaturist for the French paper *Le journal pour rire*. Wood-engraving was his preferred medium at the time. In the late 1840s and early 1850s, he made several text comics, like *Les Travaux d'Hercule* (1847), *Trois artistes incompris et mécontents* (1851), *Les Dés-agréments d'un voyage d'agrément* (1851) and *L'Histoire de la Sainte Russie* (1854).

An in-demand artist, Doré subsequently went on to win commissions to depict scenes from books by Cervantes, Rabelais, Balzac, Milton, and Dante. He also illustrated *"Gargantua et Pantagruel"* in 1854

Doré's work on The Raven was his last published work and one he never saw in print having died the year before it's publication in 1884.

# EDGAR ALLEN POE

**Edgar Allan Poe** was a writer, poet, editor, and literary critic. Poe is best known for his poetry and short stories, particularly his tales of mystery and the macabre, One of the country's earliest short story writers, Poe is also generally considered the inventor of the detective genre with *The Murders in the Rue Morgue* and *Gold Bug* being the first stories which used an investigator as the protagonist. Struggling to live on his writing alone, Poe lived most of his life in poverty..

Poe was born in Boston, the second child of actors David and Elizabeth "Eliza" Poe. His father abandoned the family in 1810, and his mother died the following year. Poe was taken in by John and Frances Allan of Richmond, Virginia. They never formally adopted him, but he was with them well into young adulthood. Poe attended the University of Virginia but left after a year due to lack of money.

His work forced him to move among several cities, including Baltimore, Philadelphia, and New York City. He married his 13-year-old cousin, Virginia Clemm, in 1836, who later died of tuberculosis in 1847. In January 1845, Poe published his poem *The Raven* to instant success. He planned for years to produce his own journal *The Penn* (later renamed *The Stylus*), but he died before it could be produced.

Poe's death Baltimore on October 7, 1849, is surrounded in as much mystery as one of his stories. . The cause of his death is unknown and has been variously attributed to disease, alcoholism, substance abuse, suicide, and other causes. He and his work appear throughout popular culture in literature, music, films, and television. **The Mystery Writers of America** present an annual award known as the *Edgar Award* for distinguished work in the mystery genre.

And the Raven, never flitting, still is sitting, still is sitting
On the pallid bust of Pallas just above my chamber door;
And his eyes have all the seeming of a demon's that is dreaming,
And the lamplight o'er him streaming throws his shadow on the floor;
And my soul from out that shadow that lies floating on the floor
Shall be lifted—nevermore!

"Be that word our sign in parting, bird or fiend," I shrieked, upstarting-
"Get thee back into the tempest and the Night's Plutonian shore!
Leave no black plume as a token of that lie thy soul hath spoken!
Leave my loneliness unbroken!—quit the bust above my door!
Take thy beak from out my heart, and take thy form from off my door!"
Quoth the Raven, "Nevermore."

"Prophet!" said I, "thing of evil—prophet still, if bird or devil!
By that Heaven that bends above us—by that God we both adore-
Tell this soul with sorrow laden if, within the distant Aidenn,
It shall clasp a sainted maiden whom the angels name Lenore-
Clasp a rare and radiant maiden whom the angels name Lenore."
Quoth the Raven, "Nevermore."

"Prophet!" said I, "thing of evil!—prophet still, if bird or devil!-
Whether Tempter sent, or whether tempest tossed thee here ashore,
Desolate yet all undaunted, on this desert land enchanted-
On this home by horror haunted—tell me truly, I implore-
Is there—is there balm in Gilead?—tell me—tell me, I implore!"
Quoth the Raven, "Nevermore."

G. Doré

Then methought the air grew denser, perfumed from an unseen censer
Swung by Seraphim whose footfalls tinkled on the tufted floor.
"Wretch," I cried, "thy God hath lent thee—by these angels
he hath sent thee
Respite—respite and nepenthe, from thy memories of Lenore!
Quaff, oh quaff this kind nepenthe and forget this lost Lenore!"
Quoth the Raven, "Nevermore."

G. Doré

This I sat engaged in guessing, but no syllable expressing
To the fowl whose fiery eyes now burned into my bosom's core;
This and more I sat divining, with my head at ease reclining
On the cushion's velvet lining that the lamplight gloated o'er,
But whose velvet violet lining with the lamplight gloating o'er,
She shall press, ah, nevermore!

But the Raven still beguiling all my fancy into smiling,
Straight I wheeled a cushioned seat in front of bird, and bust and door;
Then upon the velvet sinking, I betook myself to linking
Fancy unto fancy, thinking what this ominous bird of yore-
What this grim, ungainly, ghastly, gaunt and ominous bird of yore
Meant in croaking "Nevermore."

Startled at the stillness broken by reply so aptly spoken,
"Doubtless," said I, "what it utters is its only stock and store,
Caught from some unhappy master whom unmerciful Disaster
Followed fast and followed faster till his songs one burden bore-
Till the dirges of his Hope that melancholy burden bore
Of 'Never—nevermore'."

Much I marvelled this ungainly fowl to hear discourse so plainly,
Though its answer little meaning—little relevancy bore;
For we cannot help agreeing that no living human being
Ever yet was blest with seeing bird above his chamber door-
Bird or beast upon the sculptured bust above his chamber door,
With such name as "Nevermore."

But the raven, sitting lonely on the placid bust, spoke only
That one word, as if his soul in that one word he did outpour.
Nothing further then he uttered—not a feather then he fluttered-
Till I scarcely more than muttered, "other friends have flown before-
On the morrow he will leave me, as my hopes have flown before."
Then the bird said, "Nevermore."

Then this ebony bird beguiling my sad fancy into smiling,
By the grave and stern decorum of the countenance it wore.
"Though thy crest be shorn and shaven, thou," I said,
"art sure no craven,
Ghastly grim and ancient raven wandering from the Nightly shore-
Tell me what thy lordly name is on the Night's Plutonian shore!"
Quoth the Raven, "Nevermore."

Open here I flung the shutter, when, with many a flirt and flutter,
In there stepped a stately raven of the saintly days of yore;
Not the least obeisance made he; not a minute stopped or stayed he;
But, with mien of lord or lady, perched above my chamber door-
Perched upon a bust of Pallas just above my chamber door-
Perched, and sat, and nothing more

Back into the chamber turning, all my soul within me burning,
Soon again I heard a tapping somewhat louder than before.
"Surely," said I, "surely that is something at my window lattice:
Let me see, then, what thereat is, and this mystery explore-
Let my heart be still a moment and this mystery explore;-
'Tis the wind and nothing more."

G. Doré

Deep into that darkness peering, long I stood there wondering, fearing,
Doubting, dreaming dreams no mortals ever dared to dream before;
But the silence was unbroken, and the stillness gave no token,
And the only word there spoken was the whispered word, "Lenore!"
This I whispered, and an echo murmured back the word, "Lenore!"-
Merely this, and nothing more.

Presently my soul grew stronger; hesitating then no longer,
  "Sir," said I, "or Madam, truly your forgiveness I implore;
But the fact is I was napping, and so gently you came rapping,
And so faintly you came tapping, tapping at my chamber door,
That I scarce was sure I heard you"—here I opened wide the door;-
  Darkness there, and nothing more.

And the silken sad uncertain rustling of each purple curtain
Thrilled me—filled me with fantastic terrors never felt before;
So that now, to still the beating of my heart, I stood repeating,
"'Tis some visitor entreating entrance at my chamber door-
Some late visitor entreating entrance at my chamber door;-
This it is, and nothing more."

G. Doré

Ah, distinctly I remember it was in the bleak December,
And each separate dying ember wrought its ghost upon the floor.
Eagerly I wished the morrow;—vainly I had sought to borrow
From my books surcease of sorrow—sorrow for the lost Lenore-
For the rare and radiant maiden whom the angels name Lenore-
Nameless here for evermore.

Once upon a midnight dreary, while I pondered, weak and weary,
Over many a quaint and curious volume of forgotten lore,
While I nodded, nearly napping, suddenly there came a tapping,
As of some one gently rapping, rapping at my chamber door.
"'Tis some visitor," I muttered, "tapping at my chamber door-
Only this, and nothing more."

NEVERMORE

G. Doré